# CAREER CONFIDENCE

# WORKBOOK

## Strategies to Build Your CAREER With Confidence

### JILL J. JOHNSON, MBA

**Based off insight from the international award-winning book:**
*Compounding Your Confidence*

# CAREER CONFIDENCE

# WORKBOOK

## Strategies to Build Your CAREER With Confidence

**JILL J. JOHNSON, MBA**

Based off insight from the international award-winning book:
*Compounding Your Confidence*

# Career Confidence Workbook:
## Strategies to Build Your Career With Confidence

Copyright © 2020 Jill J. Johnson

Published by Johnson Consulting Services
Minneapolis, Minnesota
www.jcs-usa.com

Book Edited by Jan McDaniel

Book Design by Chris Mendoza, CAMM. arts LLC.

For information on Jill or on how to order bulk copies of any of her books or this workbook, contact her at: www.jcs-usa.com

ISBN 978-0-9984236-7-8

1. Business   2. Self-Help   3. Non-Fiction

Printed in the United States of America

# Author's Note

This is a work of creative nonfiction. The advice offered here and the questions provided are solely intended to stimulate your thinking about how you can take control and influence your career.

**This book is dedicated to the
many young professionals I have
mentored over the years.**

You have inspired me. You have encouraged me to stretch my thinking and learn new ways to achieve excellence. I have walked the winding road to success with you and watched how you have weathered the challenges seeking success inevitably brings. I look forward to the exciting possibilities of your leadership. Thank you for trusting me and sharing your dreams for success with me. I am so proud of you all.

# Career Confidence Workbook:
## Strategies to Build Your Career With Confidence

# Contents

# Chapter 1
# Confidence Building is Your Life's Journey

Most people believe that you are born with confidence—either you have it, or you don't. This self-limiting belief is why so many people hold themselves back from ever reaching their true potential. Developing confidence is a significant life skill. It is also an essential core competency that's necessary to achieve any level of success.

Confidence can be elusive as we journey through life and our careers. Doubt, low self-esteem, and a lack of emotional control undermine our ability to deal with adversity or failure and limits our willingness to take the actions necessary for success.

What if there was a way for you to build your confidence? What if you could learn how to believe in yourself so you could leverage all your skills and talents? What if you could make a difference in your community or become a leader within your organization?

You can – if you take responsibility for building your own confidence. You need to constantly practice your skills. The cumulative impact of small and focused efforts to build your skills will increase your confidence over time. As your confidence compounds, you'll find you can achieve vastly more than you ever dreamed was possible.

Each stage of your personal growth requires a new foundation of confidence to ensure your success. The foundation for your confidence is built by your daily choices, the efforts you make, and the actions you take. You build your confidence by moving from one step to the next.

The exercises in this workbook will help you hone your confidence so it will be a constant, reliable partner as you make your way through the peaks and valleys of your career. Let's dive deeper into the critical elements of how you can begin Compounding Your Confidence.

# Describe 3 times when you did <u>not</u> feel confident

**Where were you? Why didn't you feel confident in this situation?**

**What could have you done differently to have been more confident in this situation?**

1.

2.

3.

# Describe 3 times when you felt confident

Where were you?                    Describe why you felt confident.

1.

2.

3.

# CAREER CONFIDENCE

*"Most people believe that you are born with confidence—either you have it, or you don't. This self-limiting belief is why so many people hold themselves back from ever reaching their true potential."*

– Jill J. Johnson

Notes:

# Chapter 2
## Clarify Your Confidence Timeline

Everyone has to move through different levels of confidence. You have to figure out your baseline of where you are starting from now. Then you can expand your options to identify your next level of future opportunities. Through this exercise, you will learn to take risks to let your confidence compound so you can move to new levels of success. You must be willing to learn how to turn one success into another and another.

Begin with developing a timeline of your life. This timeline will help you reflect on how much growth you have already achieved. Think about the major periods of time in your life. What were you doing when you were the age of 18? What experiences in work and leadership did you engage in when you were a young adult? Did you get married and have children? Did you attend college or another educational institution? Did you go straight into a fulltime job?

One common theme among successful people is they all have doubts. They are often afraid they may fail; but they succeed because they hone their skills through their successes, mistakes, and failures. They learn from their experiences and focus on how they can do better next time. With each successive effort, they built their skill progressions and gained confidence. You can too.

Everyone who achieves success leverages their talents and develops new skills. They also put in the effort to gain confidence in their abilities. The same thing holds true for you too.

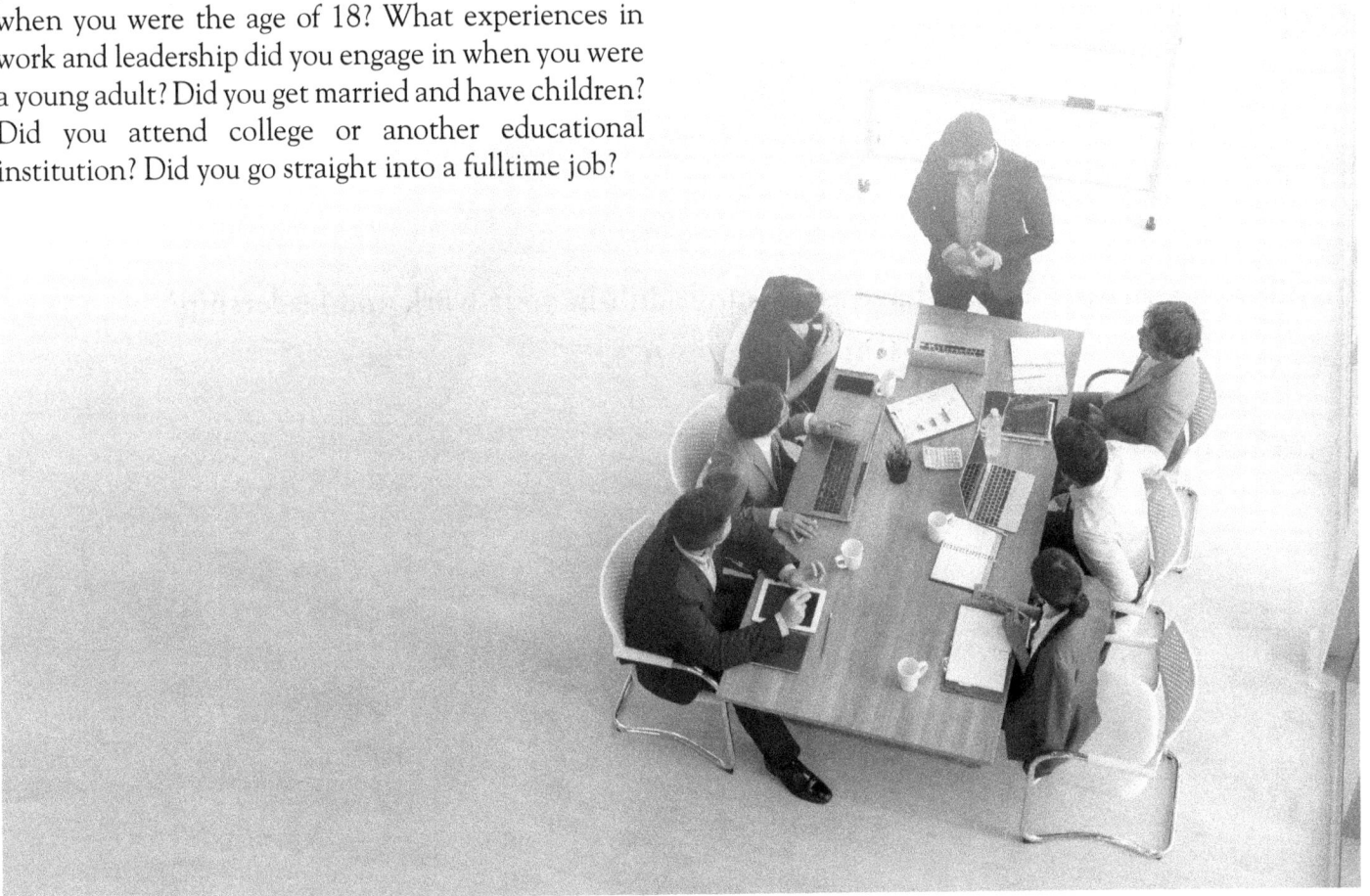

1. What were you doing when you were a teenager? What were you learning from those you were connecting with at home, work, school, etc.?

2. What were you doing when you were ages 18 to 22? What were you learning from those you were connecting with at home, work, school, etc.?

3. What experiences did you have as a young adult in your work and leadership?

**Your Timeline History:** Reflect about an early period in your professional life or school experiences. What successes and challenges did you experience? Did that experience prepare you for the job you have now or the one you desire? Did you obtain a solid foundation of education and experience for your next opportunity? Or, do you need to work on that first? This reflection will help identify where you need to begin. Take some time and reflect on the following questions.

1. What have been the 3 to 5 major milestones in your life?

2. What have been the key elements that allowed you to establish some level of success as you have moved from your early career to today?

3. Did you believe you deserved to achieve this success? Why or why not?

## CAREER CONFIDENCE

*"Everyone who achieves a high level of success at some point decided it was right for her or him to achieve it. You have to ask yourself 'Why not me?'"*

– Jill J. Johnson

Notes:

_____

_____

_____

_____

_____

_____

_____

_____

_____

_____

_____

_____

# Chapter 3

# Develop Your Personal SWOT

In the business world, as part of the strategic planning process, organizations evaluate their strengths, weaknesses, opportunities, and threats. This is called a SWOT Analysis, using the first initials of each word.

A SWOT Analysis is a framework for leaders of an organization to consider all of the internal and external factors impacting their enterprise. They use this process to consider all of their options for moving forward to resolve issues, leverage their strengths and make critical decisions to improve their success.

Developing a Personal SWOT Analysis is important to your professional growth. Evaluate your personal strengths, weaknesses, opportunities and threats. Be honest! Your SWOT Analysis is a snapshot of where you are right now and can help you plan your future growth.

What **strengths** can you build on? What **weaknesses** can you work to overcome – and how will you overcome them?

Identify the **opportunities** you can seize, or create, to enhance your success. We often don't see the opportunities right in front of us. Thinking deeply about opportunities will give you clarity about how you can move forward. Evaluate the time, effort and money you'll need to invest to take advantage of your available opportunities.

Consider the potential **threats** you could be facing. Are you limiting your success – or are there outside forces limiting your potential? Identify ways you can minimize the impact of these threats. You can take action to ensure you have the education, professional credentials or certifications you need to move forward in your career. You can change a perception people have about your skills by intentionally working on developing them.

Be sure to ask others who know you well for their feedback on each of these areas. Compare their responses with your own. Engaging in a Personal SWOT Analysis is a powerful technique for gaining insight and confidence. Do this periodically and you'll have a good sense of your progression and what to focus on next.

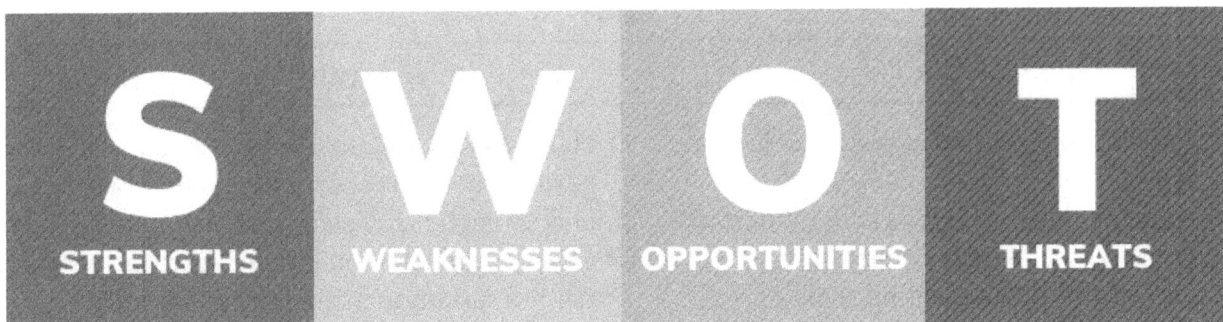

# S W O T
**STRENGTHS** **WEAKNESSES** **OPPORTUNITIES** **THREATS**

Here are two examples:

| BUSINESS SWOT SAMPLE | |
|---|---|
| **Strengths** | **Weaknesses** |
| • Excellent Staff<br>• Clear niche in who we serve<br>• Excellent educational programs<br>• Sales great but cyclical<br>• Strong financials<br>• Strong camaraderie among our team | • Staff time compressed due to business demands<br>• Geographic dispersion of our clients<br>• Generational differences among staff<br>• Not the only game in town for what we sell<br>• Marketing is not effectively messaging to our clients<br>• Limited benefits impact hiring employees |
| **Opportunities** | **Threats** |
| • Need to unearth new talents within our staff<br>• Brag more about what we offer – tell our story better<br>• Expand the geographic area we serve<br>• Better leverage remote learning options<br>• Bigger presence with social media<br>• Improve back office support | • Retirement of our older team members without having team fully trained to replace them (institutional knowledge)<br>• Overly dependent on key revenue streams – need more revenue diversity<br>• Seasonality of our sales<br>• Labor shortage<br>• Recession potential |

| PERSONAL SWOT SAMPLE | |
|---|---|
| **Strengths** | **Weaknesses** |
| • Excellent ability to work independently<br>• Highly coachable – only have to give her correction or insight on how to do it better once and she runs with it<br>• Highly organized<br>• Excellent editing skills<br>• Listens well<br>• Gaining confidence in speaking up<br>• Exceptionally intelligent<br>• Excellent listening skills | • Lack of experience – this will come with time<br>• Personality varies with mood<br>• Not always aware of how she is being perceived by others (or does not care)<br>• Prefers to work independently<br>• Always looking for the next best thing – not always mindful of how this comes across to others<br>• Writes without intention or clarity |
| **Opportunities** | **Threats** |
| • Very mature and presents more maturely than she is<br>• Strong networking ability is a skill set that will benefit her ability to achieve her goals<br>• Strong written communication skills<br>• Ability to self-manage is a key skill set that will provide many opportunities | • Her preference for solo work may limit her advancement as career will require her to work with and through many other people, including clients<br>• Overly dependent on getting approval from others – hard to sustain in a rapid-paced workplace |

# Complete Your SWOT Analysis:

Honestly identify your personal strengths, weaknesses, opportunities, and threats (SWOT) that may impact your potential for achieving the success you desire in both your personal and professional life. Ask others who know you well for their feedback about your SWOT too.

## STRENGTHS

**What are your top 3 strengths?**     **How are you using them?**

1.

2.

3.

# WEAKNESSES

**What are your top 3 weaknesses?**　　　　**How are you addressing/improving them?**

1.

2.

3.

# OPPORTUNITIES

**What opportunities do you have available?**     **How are you taking advantage of them?**

1.

2.

3.

# THREATS

**What are your biggest threats to success?**          **How are you minimizing the impact?**

1.

2.

3.

**Summarize Your Personal SWOT:** Now sit down with a trusted friend or advisor to go over their thoughts on your SWOT. Does your view of yourself match their assessment? Did you gain some new insights? Summarize your revised thinking of your Personal SWOT based on your conversation.

| YOUR PERSONAL SWOT | |
|---|---|
| **Strengths** | **Weaknesses** |
| | |
| **Opportunities** | **Threats** |
| | |

*"As you see the greater possibilities for your life, you will begin searching to make them real. As you do this, you will build more confidence, and the sky can be your limit."*

– Jill J. Johnson

Notes:

# Chapter 4

# The 3 Keys to Building Your Confidence

There are three keys to building your confidence: progressions, practice, and presentation. Each provides you with the foundation necessary to move forward with confidence. They also offer the insight you will need to regroup when your confidence fails.

**Progressions** means layering your skills over time so you develop deeper levels of refinement. Few people understand the importance of deliberately breaking down their skill development into smaller bite-size chunks. Most people try to work on too many things at once. By concentrating on smaller focus areas, you can more effectively build your skills. As you refine your skills through progressions, you'll find yourself gaining confidence as you move from one level of mastery to the next.

**Practice** is essential to being able to rely on a skill. As you practice the various elements of it over and over, you'll gain confidence in your abilities.

Mastering a skill does not happen overnight or by engaging in it a few times. With any skill, you'll need to practice in many different venues and situations before it will become something you can execute with consistency.

**Presentation** means stepping forward to allow others to see how well you can perform your skills. As you improve your skills, you will become more confident. Then you'll project your well-earned confidence to others and you'll present yourself with greater credibility.

The first step is to identify the skill you need to develop to move toward whatever is your next level of success. Ask yourself if you can improve even more on a skill you're already good at. Is there something else you need to learn so you can demonstrate that skill flawlessly when you are under pressure? Next determine how you are going to intentionally build this skill and start working on it.

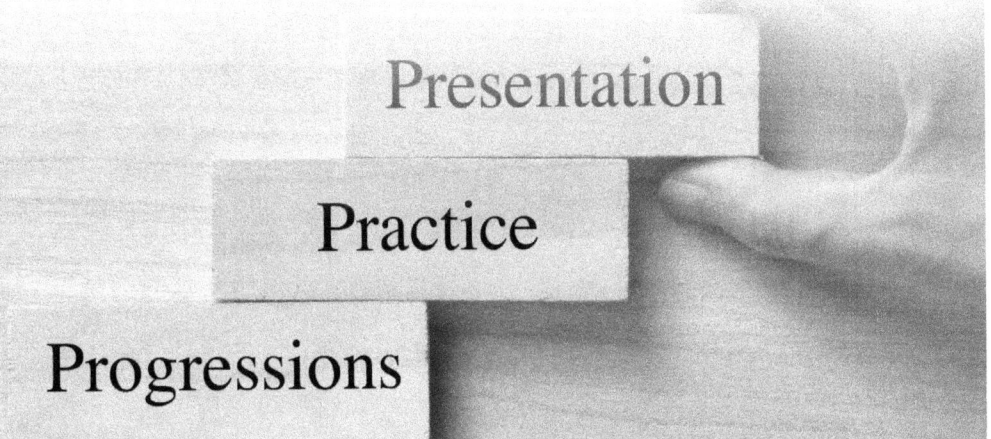

Presentation

Practice

Progressions

1. What skill(s) do you already have some level of expertise in that with further refinement could help you be more successful?

2. What other skill(s) should you develop to be more successful?

3. How do you want to use these skills in your future?

**CAREER CONFIDENCE**

*"Keep in mind confidence is a skill. As with any new skill, you must practice it over and over for it to become something you can do with ease."*

– Jill J. Johnson

Notes:

**Notes:**

# Chapter 5

# Build Your Confidence Through Progressions

One way to build your confidence is through progressions. This means continuously layering your skills over time to develop deeper levels of refinement. As you refine your skills, you'll progress from one level of success to the next. Your progressions become the foundation of your confidence.

To develop any skill, you master it through learning in incremental progressions. It's easier to focus if you break it down into smaller bites, so you can understand how to improve each aspect of the skill.

For example, in gymnastics, after you learn a cartwheel on the floor, you learn to do it on a balance beam. Taking incremental steps, mastered over time, and then – voila! – you can do a cartwheel on the high balance beam without using your hands, just like an Olympic champion.

You go through the same progressions in building any skill you need to advance your career.

Whether it's public speaking, making a big sale or developing a strategic plan, every skill is learned based on progressions. With each progression, you overcome your fear. As you lose your fear, you gain confidence in your ability. You develop trust in yourself. As you trust yourself, you gain more confidence. Then you can address the details of refining the skill to increase your finesse.

As you develop confidence, it starts to show in your performance. As it shows in your performance, you move to a whole new level of ability and mastery. Confidence results in awards, promotions, new opportunities, and greater success. Write down the progressions for the skills you need to work on. Then work on them!

# Progressions Build Your Skills:

Confidence is a skill. Just as with any new skill, you must practice it over and over for it to become something you can do with ease. The key is to clarify which skill you need to build on so you can master it.

1. Narrow your focus to pick one skill that you most need to develop to move to your next level of success. Be specific.

2. Why is this specific skill important to your personal or professional development?

3. What is your goal for developing this skill?

**4.** What action steps do you need to take to improve this skill?

**5.** What resources do you need to move this forward? Identify the time, money, coaches/mentors, or other resources this will take for you to be successful.

**6.** When is your timeline for completion for this? Are there interim checkpoints?

# CAREER CONFIDENCE

*"Life is about moving forward. It's about the inner component deep within you encouraging you to find a way to overcome your fears to achieve your goals and create the life you desire."*

– Jill J. Johnson

Notes:

# Chapter 6
## Building Your Confidence Requires Practice

You know the saying, "Luck is what happens when preparation meets opportunity." It's so true. If you're not prepared, you won't have confidence in yourself when the opportunity to move forward toward your dreams presents itself. Building your confidence requires practice. There are no shortcuts. Effective practice takes consistent work, over time.

Always be preparing and practicing, so you develop your skills before you need them. Practicing a skill is essential before you can rely on it without thinking. Work on your skills in small bites so you don't get overwhelmed by trying, and failing, at multiple big things.

Finding opportunities to practice new skills are all around you. You should plan to practice your new skills both inside and outside of work. Be on the lookout for every opportunity to practice.

You can practice your skill development anywhere— in the office, at school or in a church group. You can even practice your skills while you are interacting with your children, shopping at the grocery store or coaching soccer.

Volunteering will give you opportunities to practice your skills too, such as speaking up with confidence or watching how others use their skills to advance an idea.

Even practice your self-talk so you are shaping your confidence mindset with positive messages. Come up with a motivating mantra. This is a phrase you can say to yourself repeatedly for encouragement. Say it as if you know you will achieve it. A positive mantra will work for you.

Practicing new skills consistently builds your confidence and is essential to achieving the success you want and deserve.

# Find Opportunities to Practice: Opportunities to practice new skills are all around you. You should plan to practice your new skills both inside and outside of school or work. What can move you forward? Be bold in your ideas!

1. **Volunteer Experience:** Where can you find assignments that will get you in front of more people and allow you to practice your skills?

2. **Agree to Do Something:** What can you say "yes" to that will help you practice your new skill? What assignment can you take on or what committee can you join?

3. **Ask for It:** What can you tell people you want to work on next? Who do you have to ask? How will you approach them to ask for it?

**4. Apply for It:** What can you put your hat in the ring for? Can you submit for an award? Can you apply for a new job or a promotion?

**5. Say it Out Loud:** What do you need to practice saying so you can get comfortable saying the words before you need to say it in front of someone else? Where will you practice this?

**6. What else can you do to practice?**

*"Don't psych yourself out of discovering your potential. Be open to becoming more than you think you are capable of today."*

– Jill J. Johnson

**Notes:**

# Chapter 7
# The Importance of Volunteering

Confidence is a significant life skill you develop through practice. Volunteering with a nonprofit organization or in a business or professional association are excellent ways to practice your skills. They offer opportunities and assignments that expose you to more people, wider perspectives, and a variety of chances to augment your experience.

Confidence will come to you faster when you practice in a relatively low-risk environment such as volunteering with an association. The ultimate stakes will not be as high there as when you are only practicing the skill in your day job.

By agreeing to serve in a volunteer leadership role, you'll have an opportunity to practice your new skills. Then you get to take the skills you develop in this voluntary leadership role back into your workplace. This allows you to progress at a much more rapid pace.

Just showing up is one thing, but isn't nearly enough. To be an effective volunteer, actively put your skills to work for the organization or association. Volunteer for projects and follow through. You are practicing and perfecting your skills; at the same time, you are helping move the volunteer organization's strategies forward. People will notice.

You're probably thinking you are too busy to serve on a board or volunteer for a committee role. This is taking a very narrow viewpoint and limits your opportunities. There's no better way to spend your time than helping a worthy organization progress while simultaneously building your own skills and confidence.

Volunteer leadership experience and the confidence you develop through these activities can have an exceptional impact on your entire career.

1. List several organizations or professional groups that you might enjoy volunteering with that would be aligned with your success goals.

2. Which one of these organizations is going to most directly contribute to your next level of success? Why?

3. What will you gain from this volunteering activity?

**4. What skills can you contribute to the organization?**

**5. How much time are you willing to invest?**

**6. Who should you tell that you want to do this? How will you make your desired involvement a reality?**

## CAREER CONFIDENCE

*"Volunteer leadership experience can have an exceptional impact on your entire career."*

– Jill J. Johnson

**Notes:**

# Chapter 8
# Present Yourself Confidently

Confidence fuels your desires and big goals. Unfortunately, you need more than fuel to achieve success. Beyond preparing, you need to allow others to observe your potential. This means you need to become comfortable with allowing people to see you in action.

Successful people are not invisible. They do not hide in the shadows. It is hard to get comfortable with learning how to present yourself confidently in front of others. Presenting yourself confidently requires self-trust. Here are several actions you can take to present yourself with more confidence:

- **Be Visible:** Let people see you. It takes tons of practice to become comfortable standing in front of others. It takes consistent practice in many different arenas to build your confidence so you can trust yourself enough to stand alone in the spotlight in front of peers, bosses or strangers.

- **Body Language:** Your posture and facial expressions play an important role in helping you project confidence. You need to look, act, and speak with self-assurance. People who project confident body language are listened to more carefully. So, stand tall, maintain eye contact, have a strong handshake and sit up straight when you speak. This will convey an air of confidence.

- **Be Consistent:** Everything you're doing is building your personal brand. It's in how you deliver what you do. It's in the consistency of how you deliver it. It's even in how you present yourself.

One other critical aspect of your personal brand is how you deal with your emotions. As you learn to manage your emotions, you'll gain emotional maturity. This will enhance how you present your confidence to others, especially during stressful times.

**Be Visible:** Are you willing to allow people to see you and the skills you are building? If not, what will it take for you to do this?

1. How can you put this into practice?

2. What will you do when you are nervous if others notice you?

3. List 3 opportunities you can take advantage of to be more visible.

**Body Language:** You need to look, act and speak with confidence and clarity. People who project confident body language are listened to more carefully. Standing tall or sitting up straight when you speak conveys an air of confidence. What do you need to work on to polish your Executive Presence?

**1. How can you practice more confident body language?**

**2. How can you make sure you handle or control your emotions?**

**3. How can you practice speaking more confidently?**

**Be Consistent:** Everything you do conveys a message about yourself. Being consistent in those messages is important to allowing others to develop confidence in you. What do you need to work on to be more consistent?

**1. Are you consistent in all aspects of how you present yourself to others?**

**2. Are you consistent in the quality of your efforts, your preparation, and maintaining your connections?**

**3. How can you build more consistency in the quality of what you do with your skills?**

**Fear:** What are you most afraid of that stops you from seeking out new opportunities and working to achieve the success you dream of? What do you need to do to create a supportive environment to help you move through your fear? Who do you need to bring into your life to encourage you to keep moving forward toward achieving your vision and goals?

**Role Models:** Who are your role models who keep their cool no matter how much pressure they must feel? How will you work on maintaining your steady breathing no matter what is going on around you, like they do?

## CAREER CONFIDENCE

*"If you want to advance, be visible. Let people see you in action. It takes practice in many different arenas to build your confidence so you can trust yourself enough to stand in the spotlight."*

– Jill J. Johnson

Notes:

# Chapter 9
## Develop Your Own Confidence Plan

Confidence is a significant skill you need to advance in life and your career. No one is born with confidence. Everyone must devote time, effort and resources to develop it.

Creating your personal Confidence Plan is essential to developing this life skill. Begin your plan by reviewing your personal timeline. Write down the springboards and roadblocks that have affected your success so far. Look for patterns. What events or people moved you forward? Where did you get stuck?

Do an honest assessment of your Personal Strengths, Weaknesses, Opportunities and Threats. Look at your SWOT Summary. You will use this assessment to create your Confidence Plan. Ask a trusted confidant to provide you with further insight.

Write down a vision of where you want to be in five, ten or twenty years. Who do you want to be? If you don't know where you want to go, or how you'll define success, how will you ever focus your efforts? Your vision will guide your plan.

Your Confidence Plan should include an honest assessment of your current skills and how they will help you achieve your vision. Identify the additional skills you need to develop so you do too. What skills will boost your marketability? Where will you practice these skills so you can perform them with confidence?

Your Confidence Plan should also include an assessment of the investments you'll need to make in your skills and how you'll find the resources to develop them.

Finally, write down the three actions you will take this year to help achieve your vision. Then implement them.

# What is Your Vision?

**1. What do you see as the vision for your future?**

**2. Who do you want to be?**

**3. How do you want people to think of you?**

# Your Future:

**1. What will your vision of success feel like, look like, and mean to you in 5 years?**

**2. In 10 years?**

**3. In 20 years?**

**4. How do you want people to remember you at the end of your life?**

# Building Your Confidence Plan

1. What are 3 actions you can take in the next 2 weeks that will help you move forward toward reaching your next level of success?

2. What are 2 actions you can take in the next 2 months that will help you move forward toward reaching your next level of success?

3. What is one other big step you can take in the next year that will help you move forward or break through to your next level of success?

**4.** What else can you leverage to help you make that breakthrough?

**5.** Are you ready to implement your Confidence Plan? Why or why not?

**6.** What else do you have to do to achieve your vision?

# CAREER CONFIDENCE

*"Develop a commitment to enhancing your skills. The more you enhance your skills, the more your confidence will grow. When you have laid a solid foundation of preparation, step into the light and let others see how you shine."*

– Jill J. Johnson

Notes:

# Chapter 10
# Confidence is Your Constant Companion

Life is about moving forward. It's about finding the inner courage deep within you to find a way to achieve your goals, despite your fear, so you can create the life you desire.

Desire is not enough. You must make it happen. Developing and compounding your confidence is *your* journey; it can't be outsourced or delegated. Confidence is not going to be gifted to you on a silver platter. You must find your own way. Take control of your destiny. Take advantage of those unexpected moments when opportunities appear for you.

Confidence, or the lack of it, will be your constant companion as you move toward achieving your goals. If you lack confidence, your career journey will not progress in ways that make you feel proud or accomplished. You'll be stuck right where you started.

Determine what calculated risks you *can* take, so you will find a way to move yourself forward toward your dreams and goals. Then take another calculated risk. Then another. Working on your confidence has a compounding effect; it feeds on itself.

What steps can you take to move yourself forward? What do you need to know and understand to give you the confidence you need so you can be a contender? Figure it out.

Next, set your goal a level higher than you think you can achieve. Don't be your own glass ceiling.

You can be confident too, if you prepare. Think big. Be bold. Take a risk. Prepare both your skills and your mindset to ensure success, no matter how *you* define it. This is the true essence of confidence.

**Take Risks:** You need to take risks to move on to bigger success!

1. **What risks will you face?**                    **What rewards could you gain?**

2. How do you define success for your next phase of life?

3. What is holding you back from reaching for it?

4. What do you envision will happen if you achieve a higher goal than you currently think is possible?

5. What would it take for you to pursue this higher goal?

**CAREER CONFIDENCE**

*"When you truly know, understand, and accept what makes you special, you will begin to believe it. Now you can move forward and act to leverage this skill to move you to the next level of success."*

– Jill J. Johnson

Notes:

# Chapter 11

# Your Mindset Impacts Your Confidence

Your mindset is essential to building confidence. A confident mindset allows you to frame your thoughts and actions in powerful ways. It will help you stay focused on building and achieving success. Your mindset also is the underlying factor that gives you the discipline needed to achieve your goals.

One way to build your Confidence Mindset is to consider how you talk to yourself. Self-talk has power. It makes your words more than an abstract goal. Using confident words helps you clarify your belief in yourself.

Make your self-talk action oriented. Focus your self-talk on the things you will say and do. Want more. Believe you deserve more. Ask for more.

Whatever your intention or goal is, say it out loud and say it like you mean it. Say it as if you know you will achieve it. This becomes your self-talk. Practice this in your car, your shower, and in your mind.

Make sure you are listening to words to build up your confidence. Negative words undermine your self-assurance. We have enough negativity in our lives. Your self-talk might be sabotaging your confidence. Stop talking to yourself this way.

When the people around you say, "You're so talented in doing XYZ," please don't respond with the, "Oh .... I Don't Deserve It .... I'm Not Special" self-talk.

Instead bask in the moment, be grateful, and allow the supportive words to become part of your spirit.

Accept the feedback as a compliment and as acknowledgment of the results of your hard work. This is how you'll build your confidence.

# Consider the focus of your self-talk.

| What are some examples of negative self-talk you engage in? | How could you make this to more positive self-talk? |
|---|---|
| 1. | |
| 2. | |
| 3. | |
| 4. | |

# Write out 5 mantras you can use to boost your confidence.

1.

2.

3.

4.

5.

**CAREER CONFIDENCE**

*"Don't psych yourself out of discovering your potential. Be open to becoming more than you think you are capable of today."*

– Jill J. Johnson

Notes:

_____

_____

_____

_____

_____

_____

_____

_____

_____

_____

_____

# Chapter 12
## Your Confidence Will Fluctuate

Confidence is the gap between our dreams and believing we can achieve them. We all get stuck at various times in our lives. We all have self-doubts. Self-doubt is poison to confidence. Self-doubt is often triggered by fear.

Fear is a powerful emotion. It's an emotion that can cause you to hold yourself back or sabotage your success.

Your confidence will fluctuate because of fear and self-doubt. In some environments, you will feel like you can conquer anything and in other places you'll feel like you should have just stayed in bed.

When this happens, something is going on deep within you. This is the time to reflect or to reach out to a trusted confidant. Allow yourself the opportunity to embrace the stillness of a momentary plateau.

Many executives, entrepreneurs and leaders have moments of sheer terror. When this happens, it is usually because something isn't working right. These leaders need to project confidence to others to prevent *their* fears from spreading throughout their organization. Yet they are still deeply concerned that the consequences of their decisions, or of the changing market forces that they cannot control, will cause them to fail. At their level, the stakes are high.

The stakes are high no matter what level you are at when you are afraid. Confidence isn't going to *magically* appear because you want it. It's going to be within you because you work for it and you look for it. You face your fears and doubts. Then you move forward to try again.

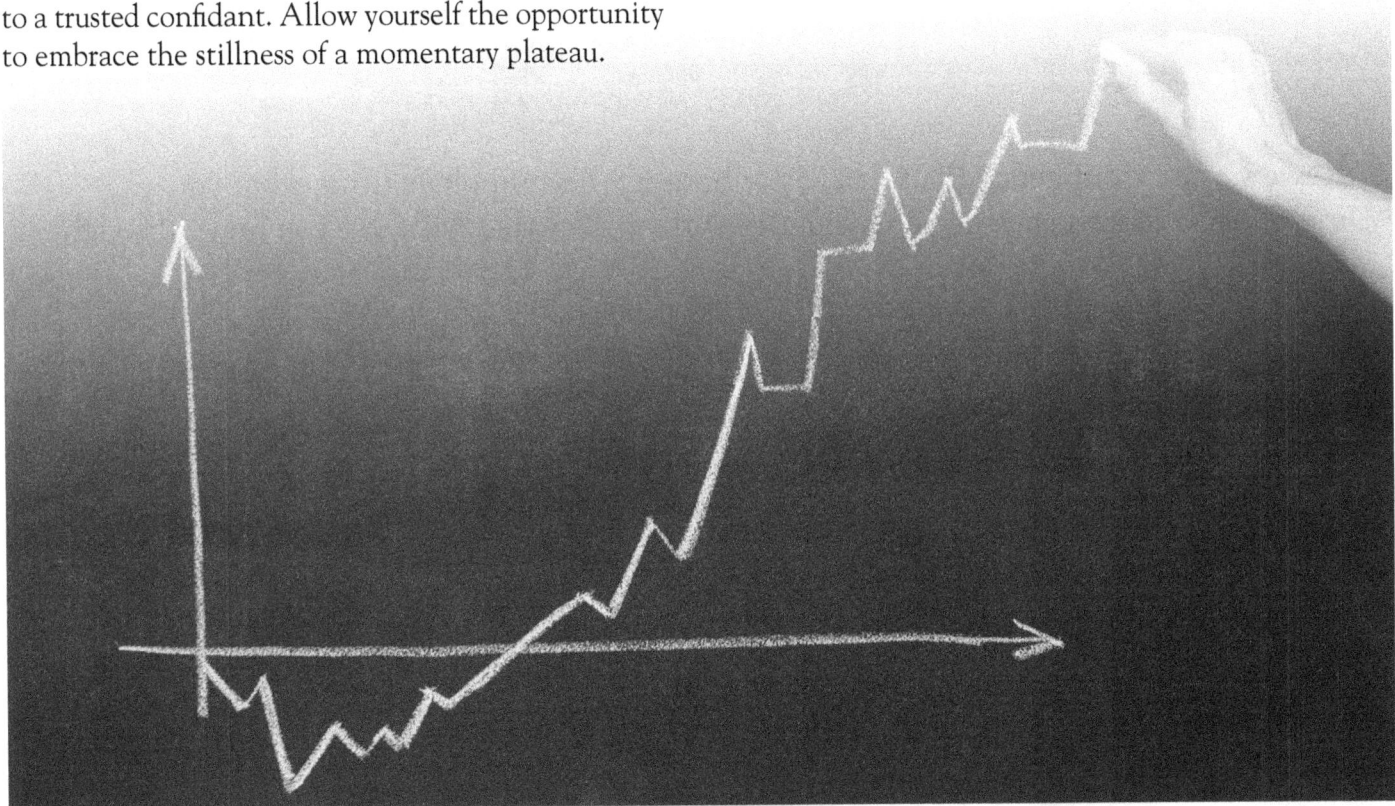

**1. What are your biggest fears that impact your potential for success?**

**2. How can you build your confidence to overcome these fears?**

**3. Review your Confidence Plan.** Have you honestly been implementing what you intended? Is there something else you can work on now that will help you move through a plateau?

*"Confidence is a significant life skill. Developing it is an essential core competency that's necessary to achieve any level of success."*

– Jill J. Johnson

Notes:

**Notes:**

# Chapter 13
## The Importance of Mentors and Coaches

Your skill development will occur in cycles. Sometimes you can't see your growth because it is so subtle. Often, we think we are at a plateau because we are not making larger moves. Then our confidence dips.

When this happens, keep in mind you are likely in a spiral of growth too slight for you to see how far you have come. Spirals feel like you are just going in circles.

We're often too close to our own actions to understand what we need to focus on for our improvement. That's why having mentors and coaches is so important to building your confidence. They can help you see the progress that exist in your spirals.

Coaches often have deeper insight about how to develop your skills as you progress through spirals. Mentors typically are already functioning at a much higher level and their wisdom can be your guide.

Coaches and mentors can help you see the nuances of what's necessary to be successful at the next level, and beyond, in your journey to building confidence. When you feel alone, doubt and fear can paralyze you from taking any action. Engaging with advisors ensures you are not alone in your efforts.

The support of these advisers can also help you do a deeper dive to identify emotional and behavioral triggers that are getting in your way. These advisers know you, care about you, and want what's best for you. They'll provide you with candid insight and offer encouragement. Take your ego out of the picture and reach out for feedback.

You should also become a mentor or coach someone else. It's an important part of confidence development to give back to those coming up behind you.

1. How has a coach or mentor helped you work through a specific issue or helped boost your confidence?

_____

2. Identify 3 people you would like to be your coach or mentor. List your reasons why you selected them.

Who?                                      Why?

_____

_____

_____

**3.** How will you approach them? How will you be specific about what you need from them? What will you offer in return?

**4.** How you will respond if they say "no" or tell you something you did not want to hear?

## CAREER CONFIDENCE

*"Don't be afraid of criticism if the advice is intended to help you become better so you perform with greater precision and skill."*

– Jill J. Johnson

Notes:

# Chapter 14
## Tips for More Confident Speaking

Public speaking can be scary – but if you're prepared and you practice, your confidence in front of audiences will grow. Here are some tips you can use.

- **Audience:** Think about who will be in the room: age, gender, profession. Then match your message to what they care about.

- **Outline:** Develop an outline for your speech. This will help you focus your content.

- **Introduction:** Your introduction should highlight the overview of the main points you will be talking about.

- **Main Topics:** Remember the Power of Three. This means you have no more than three main topics to share with your audience. Limiting yourself to three main topics provides structure to your talk.

- **Sub-Themes:** Under each of the three main topics, put together the three to five sub-themes you want to address. Each sub-theme should be relevant to the main point it falls under. Your topics and your sub-points should build on each other too.

- **Conclusion:** Don't end your speech with audience questions. Instead, as you move into your conclusion, ask your audience if they have any questions. Take the time to answer them. Then circle back and reemphasize the importance of your three main points. Leave them with a final encouraging message.

Practice your speech a minimum of four times so you get comfortable with the words. At least one of your practices should be in front of other people. Practicing will build your confidence and your jitters will subside because you are prepared.

1. Who is your audience for your upcoming speech?

2. What are the three main points you will cover in your speech?

3. Where will you execute your practice sessions? Who will you practice in front of and get feedback from?

## CAREER CONFIDENCE

*"If you want to advance, be visible. Let people see you in action. It takes practice in many different arenas to build your confidence so you can trust yourself enough to stand in the spotlight."*

– Jill J. Johnson

Notes:

# Notes:

# Chapter 15
## Be Wary of Golden Handcuffs

In the business world, "Golden Handcuffs" are the lucrative benefits employers offer as incentives to discourage employees from taking another job.

You can think of Golden Handcuffs as those thoughts holding you back from pursuing your goals. Golden Handcuffs are the psychological limits you set up that prevent you from taking the risks necessary to achieve your goals. Golden Handcuffs in your case might be the security of a paycheck or not moving from your hometown for a better opportunity.

Don't let your fears psych you out before you see what you are truly capable of achieving. Sometimes it may not be the right time for you to achieve your goal... yet. Sometimes you'll need some help to move forward. Don't let your ego get in the way of asking for the support you need.

Don't let Golden Handcuffs be the roadblock to your success. When you hold yourself back, you'll never know what you were truly capable of accomplishing. You do not have to set limits for yourself. You can move forward to take action to achieve your big dreams. Even if you don't fully reach them, it doesn't matter. What matters is that you will go farther, and you will achieve more, than if you did nothing because you held yourself back.

Don't let your self-doubt handcuff your opportunity to achieve great success. You have the potential to be transformative to your enterprise, to your community, and to your family. It is simply a matter of re-framing your mindset to tell yourself you can. Then do it!

1. **What potential Golden Handcuffs are holding you back from achieving your desired goals?**

2. **How can you overcome them or work around them?**

## CAREER CONFIDENCE

*"When you have the chance to make your dream come true, grab it with both hands. Don't let the Golden Handcuffs keep you where you are—and to hold you back from fully embracing your success."*

– Jill J. Johnson

Notes:

**Notes:**

# Chapter 16
## Decide What You Want to Accomplish

You need to know what it is you want to accomplish. This gives focus to your actions and efforts. Without focus, you can't identify exactly what skills you need to work on, the people you need to connect with, or the opportunities you'll need to challenge yourself.

When you have no focus, you're just engaging in random actions that will never propel you to success. Random actions have no patterns and they prevent you from building any momentum. Without focus, you can never develop a confidence mindset you can rely upon.

Look, we all have the same number of hours in a day. The key is to focus your efforts on the little details of the actions you take each day. Your focused effort, compounded over time, creates new habits that prepare you for increasing levels of success.

When you develop habits focused on doing better each time, this shifts your mindset. Your mindset becomes the foundation for how you conduct yourself in life and how much you can actually achieve.

Take control. Take advantage of opportunities that appear for you. Or act boldly to create new opportunities for yourself.

No matter what, keep moving forward so your confidence keeps compounding. Then reach your hand back to someone coming behind you and help build their confidence. Paying it forward always winds up helping you too.

I don't know your future, but I do know this: if you own it, act on it, and you make it yours, you will compound your confidence. You will find the path to take you on the journey to achieving your golden future.

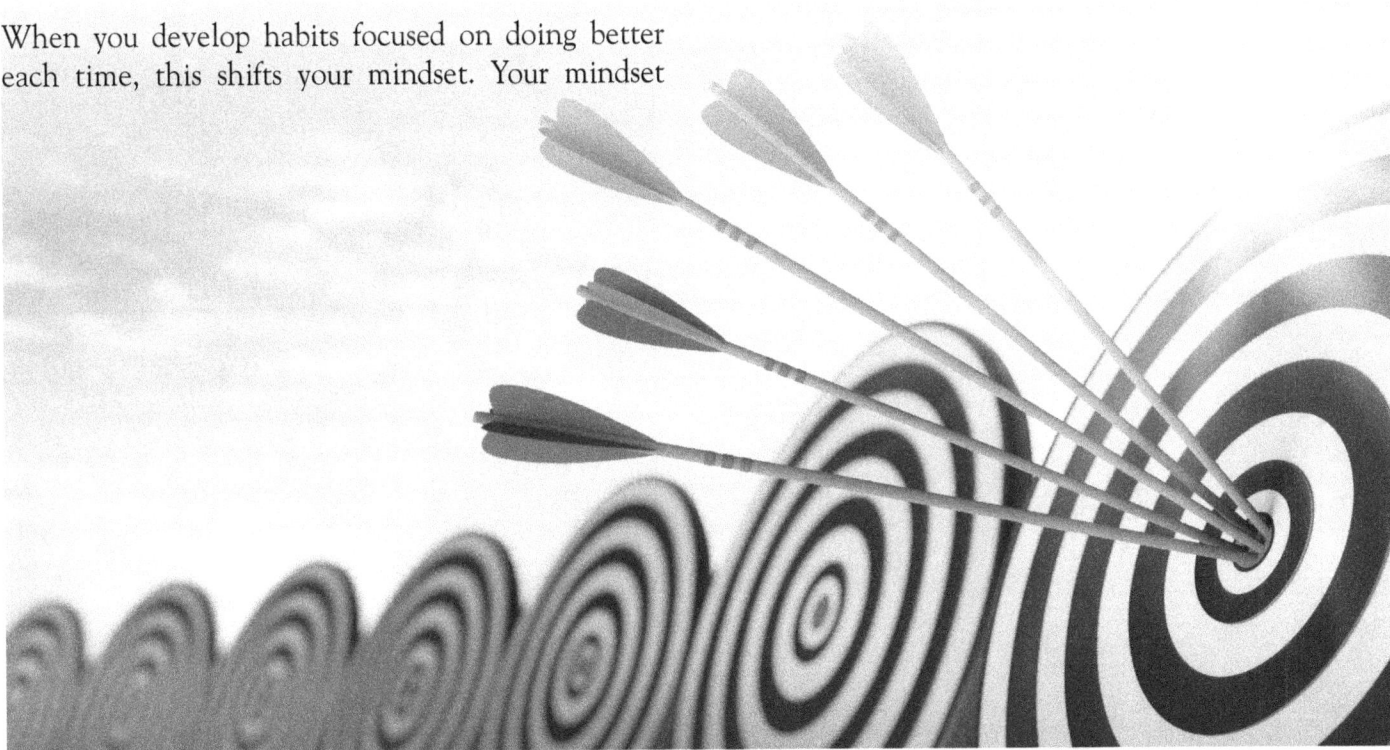

**What are 3 specific goals or achievements you want to accomplish?**

**What do you have to do to make this realistic and achievable?**

1.

2.

3.

# CAREER CONFIDENCE

*"Develop a commitment to enhancing your skills. The more you enhance your skills, the more your confidence will grow."*

— Jill J. Johnson

Notes:

# Notes:

## Chapter 17
# Final Thoughts

I wasn't born with confidence. I had to navigate confusion and uncertainty at each stage of my personal growth and development of my professional career. I did not have a silver spoon that showed me the perfect path to success. I had to work hard to earn it for myself. I had to practice, build progressions and put myself out front to let others see what I was capable of when I was afraid. The key was finding ways to build my confidence to allow me to move from one level of success to the next. I discovered you must take calculated risks so you can make these moves. You must also have a plan to build your confidence.

The gap between our dreams and believing we can achieve them is confidence. We all get stuck at various times in our lives. We all experience self-doubt. Self-doubt is poison to confidence.

Confidence is something you work on your whole life. Keep trying new things! Stay resilient, even when you think you cannot. Remember the compounded impact of taking small bold actions that do not take a lot of time can morph into amazing opportunities with the potential to transform your future. Do not waste any more time.

Take control of your destiny. Take advantage of those unexpected moments when opportunities appear for you. Act boldly to create new opportunities for yourself. No matter what, keep moving forward so your confidence keeps compounding. Then reach your hand back to help someone behind you build their confidence to join you on this success journey.

*You can, you will, you are special,*
*and you are going to succeed.*
*The next steps are yours. Take them.*

**1. Who do you want to be this time next year?**

**2. What concrete actions will you take to achieve this vision of yourself?**

**3. Who do you need to include in your efforts to achieve this vision?**

**4.** What investments do you need to make in the future to achieve this vision in terms of time, money or other resources?

**5.** What do you need to do now so you are ready to make these investments in the future?

## CAREER CONFIDENCE

*"Opportunities are all around you, if you make it a priority to look for them."*

– Jill J. Johnson

Notes:

# Notes:

**Notes:**

# Notes:

# Notes:

# Notes:

# Notes:

# About Jill J. Johnson, MBA

An award-winning management consultant, Jill J. Johnson, MBA, has personally impacted more than $4 billion of business decisions through her consulting work. She is in the board rooms, the back rooms and the executive suites where complex decisions are being made, impacting the future of clients located throughout the United States, as well as in Europe and Asia. She knows what it takes to develop and implement strategies for turnarounds or growth that get results.

Jill is a widely-respected business executive and leader who has been a member of the boards of directors and executive committees of a variety of business, professional, and governmental boards. She has served on two federal boards under three different United States presidents representing both political parties.

Jill has won numerous honors for her business acumen, her leadership savvy, mentorship skills and her entrepreneurial successes. She has also been inducted into two Business Halls of Fame. She is a 4th generation entrepreneur who grew up in a family-owned business.

Over the years, Jill has been quoted on a range of management issues in national publications including *The Wall Street Journal, The New York Times, Inc., Forbes, Money Magazine* and *Entrepreneur.* She has appeared as a thought leader on a variety of radio and television business programs. Jill's articles on strategy development and strategic marketing have appeared in more than 140 publications. Her book, *Compounding Your Confidence: Strategies to Expand Your Opportunities for Success,* has been sold throughout the world and has won numerous awards.

Jill is a powerful speaker with the rare ability to deliver substantive content in a way that is engaging and easily accessible. She is also a Professional Member of the National Speakers Association.

Jill resides in Minneapolis, Minnesota.

Talk to Jill about how her Consulting Services can help you gain the clarity you need to develop your business strategies. Book Jill to Speak at your next event. Contact her at:

www.jcs-usa.com

www.twitter.com/JillJohnsonUSA
www.facebook.com/JohnsonConsultingServices
www.linkedin.com/in/JillJohnsonUSA

# Acknowledgments

Thank you to everyone who encouraged me to share my stories and knowledge about how to build your confidence with the world. You made this workbook possible.

**To my audiences:**

Who responded so strongly to the messages contained in this workbook. Thank you for telling me how much this insight has meant to you and for encouraging me to share it with others.

**To my book team:**

Jan McDaniel, for helping me pull together my ideas as I pieced together this workbook. You always are so spot on with your advice, suggestions and feedback.

Chris Mendoza, for your design expertise and patience in turning my idea into a reality.

Austin Parrish, for assisting me in getting the printed version of the workbook to the marketplace.

**To my valued insight team:**

To the four generations of colleagues and friends who took time out of their busy days to review the various drafts of my books and worked with me to bring the *Compounding Your Confidence* and *Career Confidence* books to life. You provided me with valuable feedback to narrow the focus to the most critical information. Your responses and comments proved these concepts transcend generational divides. Each of you have provided insight that shaped this workbook. My deepest thanks to Jan McDaniel, Karen Marquardt, Maddi Meierotto, Mary Angela Baker, Morag Barrett, Dawn Bjork, Sharon Gifford, Tom Roffers, Melissa Sauser, Carolyn Vreeman, Kaylene Widgren, Seraiah Brooks, Katherine "Kat" Hunt, and Laura Ledray.

Also Available...

# Recorded Live

Listen to this live recording, of Jill Johnson's dynamic keynote presentation. You will be transported into the audience with the 400 other attendees to learn, laugh and be inspired!

**PURCHASE Your Copy NOW!**
**Bulk discounts available.**

**www.jcs-usa.com**

Also Available in the BOLD Questions Series...

# Opportunities Edition

52 questions to shape how you
take advantage of your **opportunities.**

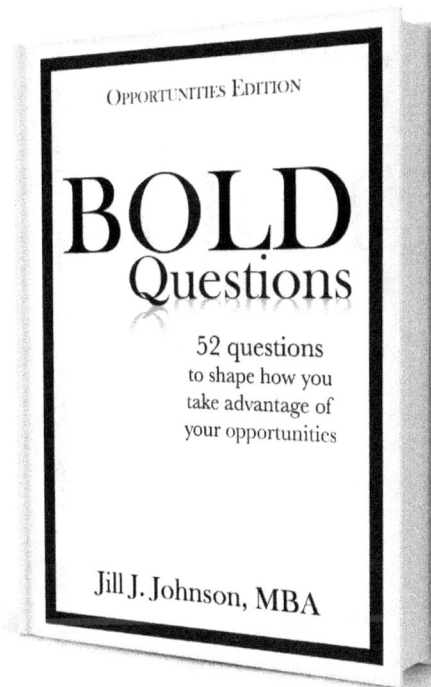

OPPORTUNITIES EDITION

# BOLD
## Questions

52 questions
to shape how you
take advantage of
your opportunities

Jill J. Johnson, MBA

## PURCHASE Your Copy NOW!
### Bulk discounts available.

**www.jcs-usa.com**

Johnson
Consulting
Services
*Marketing & Management Consultants*

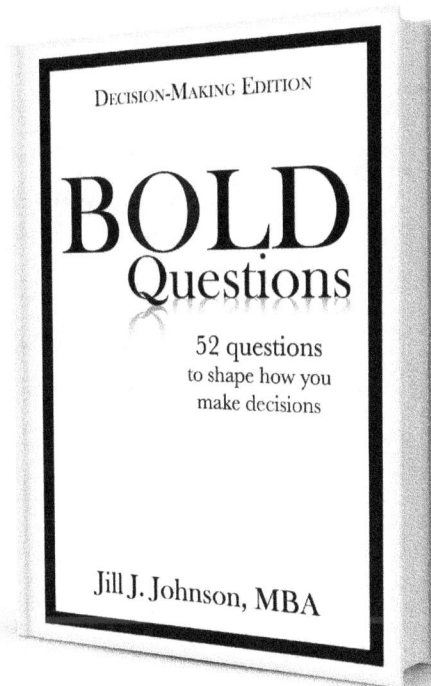

www.ingramcontent.com/pod-product-compliance
Lightning Source LLC
Chambersburg PA
CBHW051227200326
41519CB00025B/7281